SOCCER CHAMPIONS

BY JIM WHITING

LIVERPOOL FC

CREATIVE EDUCATION • CREATIVE PAPERBACKS

Published by Creative Education
and Creative Paperbacks
P.O. Box 227, Mankato, Minnesota 56002
Creative Education and Creative Paperbacks
are imprints of The Creative Company
www.thecreativecompany.us

Design and production by The Design Lab
Art direction by Rita Marshall
Printed in Malaysia

Photographs by Corbis (Ansa Archive/ANSA, Matt
Bunn/4305-4305/Colorsport, Geoff Caddick/epa,
Colorsport, Heritage Images, Hulton-Deutsch Collection,
Eddie Keogh/Reuters, Christian Liewig/Liewig Media
Sports, PHIL NOBLE/Reuters, Kai Pfaffenbach/
Reuters), Newscom (Staff/Mirrorpix), photosinbox
.com, Shutterstock (gualtiero boffi, Maxisport, Morphart
Creation, Denis Kuvaev, Olga Popova), Wikimedia
Creative Commons (Cassell's History of England published
in 1902, Jay Clark, Eric The Fish, Liverpool Football
Club, Nationaal Archief/Den Haag/Rijksfotoarchief:
Fotocollectie Algemeen Nederlands Fotopersbureau
(ANEFO), Strafpeloton2, Unknown photographer)

Library of Congress Cataloging-in-Publication Data
Whiting, Jim.
Liverpool FC / by Jim Whiting.
p. cm. — (Soccer champions)
Includes bibliographical references and index.
Summary: A chronicle of the people, matches,
and world events that shaped the European
men's English soccer team known as Liverpool
FC, from its founding in 1892 to today.
ISBN 978-1-60818-588-7 (hardcover)
ISBN 978-1-62832-193-7 (pbk)
1. Liverpool Football Club—History. I. Title.
II. Title: Liverpool Football Club.

GV943.6.L55W45 2015
796.334'640942753—dc23   2014029736

CCSS: RI.5.1, 2, 3, 8; RH.6-8.4, 5, 7

First Edition HC 9 8 7 6 5 4 3 2 1
First Edition PBK 9 8 7 6 5 4 3 2 1

Cover and page 3: Winger Raheem Sterling
Page 1: 2005 Champions League final

TABLE OF

CONTENTS

Defender Jamie Carragher

INTRODUCTION

Soccer (or football, as it is known almost everywhere else in the world) is truly a universal game. Nowhere is the play more competitive than in Europe. Almost every European country has its own league, and generally that league has several divisions. A typical season lasts eight or nine months, from late summer to mid-spring. Every team in each level plays all other teams in its level twice, once at home and once on the other team's pitch. At the end of the season, the bottommost teams in one division are relegated (moved down) to the next lower division, with the same number of topmost teams from that lower division promoted to replace them. Such a system ensures that a high level of competition is maintained and that late-season games between teams with losing records remain important as they seek to avoid relegation.

Individual countries also feature their own tournaments, such as England's FA Cup and Spain's Copa del Rey. In theory, these tournaments allow almost any team the opportunity to win the championship, but in reality the best clubs dominate the competition. An assortment of European-wide tournaments complement individual nations' league and cup play. The most prestigious is the Union of European Football Associations (UEFA) Champions League. Known as the European Cup until

Renowned players and coaches have helped England's Liverpool FC triumph as a top European contender.

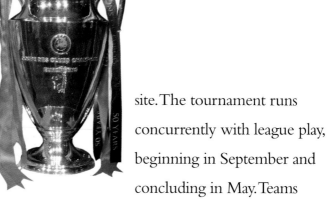

1993, the Champions League is a tournament consisting of 32 teams drawn primarily from the highest finishers in the strongest national leagues. Other teams can play their way into the tournament in preliminary rounds. It originated in 1954, when the otherwise obscure Wolverhampton Wanderers of England defeated Honved, the top-rated Hungarian side, prompting Wanderers manager Stan Cullis to declare his team "Champions of the World." Noted French soccer journalist Gabriel Hanot disagreed and helped organize a continent-wide competition that began in 1956.

The Champions League starts with eight four-team pools, which play two games with one another. The top two teams from each pool begin a series of knockout rounds, also contested on a two-game basis. The last two teams play a single championship game at a neutral site. The tournament runs concurrently with league play, beginning in September and concluding in May. Teams that win their league, their national cup, and the Champions League during the same season are said to have won the Continental Treble—almost certainly the most difficult feat in all of professional sports. The winner of the Champions League is eligible for the FIFA Club World Cup, an annual seven-team tournament that originated in 2000. It also includes teams from the Americas and Caribbean, Africa, Asia, Oceania, and the host nation.

The other major European club championship is the UEFA Europa League, founded in 1971 and known as the UEFA Cup until the 2009–10 season. The winners of these two tournaments play for the UEFA Super Cup, usually held in August.

ALL-TIME CHAMPIONS LEAGUE RECORDS OF THE TOP 10 CLUBS (AS OF 2014):

	Winner	Runner-up
Real Madrid (Spain)	10	3
AC Milan (Italy)	7	4
Bayern Munich (Germany)	5	5
Liverpool (England)	5	2
Barcelona (Spain)	4	3
Ajax (Netherlands)	4	2
Manchester United (England)	3	2
Inter Milan (Italy)	3	2
Benfica (Portugal)	2	5
Juventus (Italy)	2	5

Anfield stadium

CONTINENTAL TREBLE WINNERS

Celtic (Scotland)	1966–67
Ajax (Netherlands)	1971–72
PSV (Netherlands)	1987–88
Manchester United (England)	1998–99
Barcelona (Spain)	2008–09
Inter Milan (Italy)	2009–10
Bayern Munich (Germany)	2012–13

MACS BY THE MERSEY

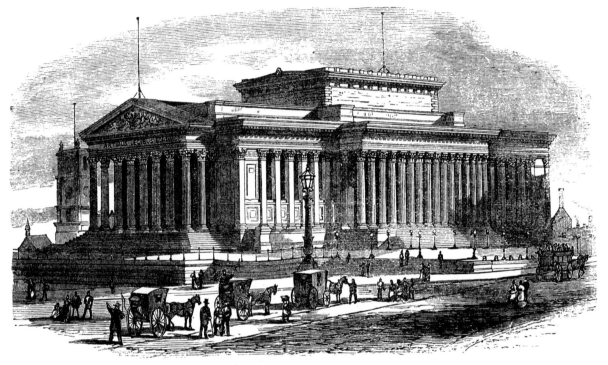

Built in the mid-1800s, St. George's Hall sits in the center of Liverpool and includes courts and concert halls.

For many people, Liverpool means one thing: the Beatles. Though John, Paul, Ringo, and George didn't arrive on the American music scene until 1964, they had already been well established in their hometown for several years. But nearly 2,000 years before the Beatles, a small group of settlers formed a village on a muddy creek called a "lifrugpool" that flowed into the River Mersey. In 1207, King John granted a charter to what was eventually known as Liverpool for the purpose of developing a seaport at the point where the Mersey emptied into the Irish Sea. By the 19th

Despite his establishment of Liverpool, King John was an unpopular ruler.

century, Liverpool had become a major English port, sending manufactured products throughout the world. After undergoing an economic depression in the latter part of the 1900s, today Liverpool is a center of music, arts, and culture as well as finance and technology.

At about the same time that King John was writing out the town's charter, the first written accounts of soccer appeared. In one form, known as "mob football," the populations of neighboring villages tried to kick inflated animal bladders toward a prominent point in the opposing village. The sport was so violent—resulting in several deaths—that kings, such as Edward II in 1314, tried to ban it. Edward IV (no relation) decreed that "No person shall practice ... football" in 1477. But not all royals felt that way. In 1526, King Henry VIII ordered a pair of soccer shoes for his personal use. According to sportswriter Vivek Chaudhary, "The version of football he played, however, was completely different from the modern game. There were no specific rules, goals, or pitch, and the game involved groups of young men kicking a heavy leather ball around a field, often sustaining serious injuries."

Fast forward to 1863, when the newly created Football Association drew up a uniform set of rules. Teams sprang up like mushrooms all over England, and Liverpool was no exception. Chief among the new clubs

Liverpool FC's newly formed "Team of all the Macs" gained attention by easily winning many of its first matches.

was Everton Football Club (FC), named for a district in the city and established in 1878. Ten years later, Everton became a founding member of the Football League, which is now the world's oldest competitive soccer league. The team's home pitch was Anfield, owned by team president John Houlding, a brewery owner (and future Liverpool mayor). The team's board of directors soon became upset with the rising rental fees Houlding charged. They also resented Houlding's monopoly on the ale that was sold at the games. The tense situation came to a head early in 1892 when the club decided to move to a new facility. Faced with the prospect of an empty field, Houlding quickly talked a group of other Everton members into founding Liverpool FC. Newly appointed manager John McKenna scoured his native Scotland for players, and the team became known as the "Team of all the Macs."

When the Football League turned down the new team's membership application, Liverpool joined the Lancashire League, an organization of teams in Lancaster County. The Liverpool club opened play on September 1, 1892, with winger Malcolm McVean scoring Liverpool's first-ever goal in a 7–1 rout of Rotherham

Town. Everton played on the same day, thereby laying the foundation for one of the most enduring rivalries in English soccer: the Merseyside Derby (a derby is a game featuring teams from the same city or region). Though the more established Everton significantly outdrew the fledglings, attendance picked up during the season as Liverpool won a treble (three championships): Lancashire League, Liverpool District Cup, and Reserve Cup. This success attracted the attention of the Football League, which reconsidered its earlier refusal and admitted Liverpool to the league's Second Division. Now the club would be playing with the big boys.

Throughout the early 20th century, Liverpool looked to position itself in the upper standings of English football.

THE REDS AND THE KOPITES

Liverpool easily won the Second Division title in its debut 1893–94 season and was promoted to the First Division. The club found the competition much tougher there, finishing 16th the following season. After being relegated back to the Second Division, Liverpool once again finished first in 1895–96. The highlight was a 10–1 romp over Rotherham, a then league record for goals scored. Center-forward George Allan scored four times in the rout, while McVean added a hat trick. Liverpool went back up to the First Division in 1896–97 and this time stayed there, winning the league title in 1900–01. Striker Sam

Raybould paced the team with 18 goals—the first of 4 times he would be the team's leading scorer during his 7 years with the club. His 130 career goals remained the team standard for 37 years.

By this time, Liverpool players had earned the nickname "Reds" based on their jersey color—which in turn reflected the official color of the city of Liverpool. Relegated again in 1903–04, the Reds won the Second Division for the third time the following season. In 1905–06, the team celebrated its return to the First Division by taking its second title. Forward Joe Hewitt had 24 league goals, while rugged Alex

Before acquiring their signature red uniforms, early Liverpool players sported blue and white colors.

LIVERPOOL

DOBSON, MOLLE & Cº EDINBURGH.

Raisbeck and keeper Sam Hardy anchored the defense. The official team website observes, "A newly promoted team winning the League Championship? It would never happen today.... Liverpool trampled over English football's aristocracy to bring the Championship back to Anfield for only the second time."

To honor that signal accomplishment and reward the growing fan base, the team built a new elevated brick terrace at one end of Anfield in 1906. It was called Spion Kop, in reference to a bloody battle during the Second Boer War (1899–1902) in which scores of English soldiers—many of whom were Liverpudlians—had been killed. Shortened to "Kop" (derived from the Dutch word for "hill"), it became

Outnumbered Boer troops took on the British at South Africa's Battle of Spion Kop in 1900 during the Second Boer War.

The increased-capacity Liverpool stadium, echoing the shape of the infamous Spion Kop hillside, invited more fans.

virtually synonymous with the name for the entire stadium, and to this day Liverpool fans are often known as Kopites.

The Kop didn't help the team's on-pitch performance. The Reds plummeted to 15th the following season and continually flirted with relegation after that. The sole highlight came on April 25, 1914, when they advanced to the finals of the FA Cup for the first time, only to lose to Burnley 1–0. A few months later, World War I began, and competition at the national level ended.

When play resumed in 1919, the team's fortunes improved. After two fourth-place finishes, the Reds took consecutive First Division titles in 1921–22 and 1922–23.

The 1919–20 Reds included scorers Jackie Sheldon, Chambers, Fred Pagnam, Forshaw, and Albert Pearson (front row, left to right).

Striker Harry Chambers paced the Reds during this era, leading them in scoring for five straight years. Perhaps his most impressive accomplishment came in a 1922 Merseyside Derby, scoring a hat trick in a 5–1 rout of the Evertonians. Fellow striker Dick Forshaw was an ideal complement in the title-winning seasons, netting 20 goals both times, while Elisha Scott was a dependable presence in goal.

Yet again, Liverpool quickly fell from the top levels. In the 16 ensuing years, the Reds managed just a pair of fourth places. It was more common to find them in the midrange, and they barely avoided relegation in the mid-1930s with back-to-back seasons of 19th and 18th place. Forward Gordon Hodgson was one of the few reasons for Kopites to be excited. The burly 6-footer from South Africa joined the team in 1925 and scored 233 league goals in his 10 years as a Red, the second-highest total in team history.

Besides Hodgson's heroics on the field, the other noteworthy development during this era came in 1928. The Kop had already become known for its vocal support of the team, and now it was expanded to accommodate up to 30,000 spectators, who remained on their feet for the entire match. It was topped with an angled iron roof, which served to amplify the already imposing amount of sound issuing from the spectators.

A little more than a decade later, an entirely different sort of sound—gunfire—would result in the second suspension of English soccer in less than a quarter of a century. On September 1, 1939, German forces invaded the neighboring nation of Poland. Nearly all of Europe—and much of the rest of the world—would soon be at war again.

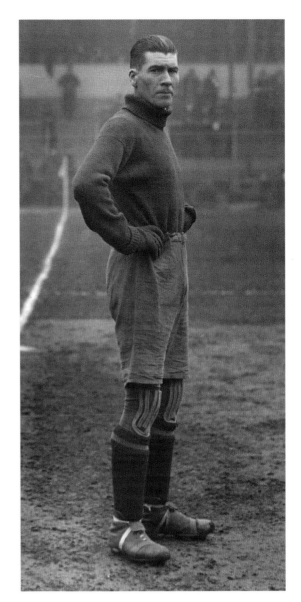

The catlike reflexes of shot-stopping Elisha Scott prompted comparisons with a panther.

A LEGEND LANDS IN LIVERPOOL

Soon after World War II ended in 1945, history repeated itself as the Reds won the 1946–47 league title only to immediately plummet downward in the standings. One of the few highlights in the next six seasons came when Liverpool finished second in the 1950 FA Cup, losing 2–0 to Arsenal in the final.

Things were even worse in 1953–54. The Reds finished dead last in the First Division and were relegated. The problem was simple: there were no reliable scorers. The team leader was striker Sammy Smyth, who only punched in 13 goals all season. Compounding the misery, the team suffered its all-time record defeat, a 9–1 December 1954 debacle against Birmingham City. This time, there was no quick rebound for the club. It was eight seasons before the Reds took first in the Second Division and were promoted once again in 1962.

The resurgence had actually begun late in 1959, when Bill Shankly took over as manager. At the time, it wasn't an obvious hire. Shankly had never managed a major club. But there could be no doubt about his passion for soccer and his

Bill Shankly reshaped Liverpool into a championship team.

Dependable center-forward Albert Stubbins was known for powerful but unselfish play.

commitment to winning. "People think football is a matter of life and death," he once said. "I assure you, it's much more serious than that."

Seeking players who shared that attitude, Shankly churned the roster. Twenty-four players departed in the first year alone. But he kept players such as striker Roger Hunt and defender Gerry Byrne, who became key members of an increasingly successful team. He also added future lineup fixtures such as winger Ian Callaghan and forward Ian St. John. The Reds finished eighth in their return from relegation in 1962–63, and then took First Division championships in 1963–64 and 1965–66. Between the two title-winning seasons, Liverpool finally ended its FA Cup drought, defeating Leeds United 2–1 in the final.

Roger Hunt (middle) battled London's Tottenham Hotspur FC players Ron Henry (left) and Cliff Jones (right).

The 1966–67 Reds took home the Charity Shield in the match between the winners of the FA Cup and the Football League.

In 1964, Manchester United midfielder Phil Chisnall joined Liverpool in a relatively minor transaction. He became the last player to transfer directly between the two powerhouses. Their rivalry—the Northwest Derby—is quite likely the most heated in English soccer. The two cities became commercial rivals in the latter years of the 19th century. By the time Chisnall arrived, they had also become the sites of the most dominant English soccer teams—first Liverpool, then Manchester. In later years, Liverpool captain Steven Gerrard typified the dislike between the two teams. He refused to follow the longtime soccer custom of swapping shirts with Manchester United after games, nor would he allow a ManU shirt in his home.

As the 1970s dawned, Shankly—by now recognized as one of the top managers in the sport—continued to add new talent to keep his team fresh. Defender Emlyn

Ian Callaghan and midfielder Peter Cormack (#8) helped the Reds take the 1973 UEFA Cup final.

Hughes and strikers John Toshack and Kevin Keegan were instrumental as the Reds won the First Division in 1972–73 and gained their first European trophy with a 3–2 victory over Germany's Borussia Mönchengladbach in the UEFA Cup. The following year, Liverpool added its second FA Cup with a 3–0 thumping of Newcastle United.

Seemingly at the apex of success, Shankly stunned Liverpool—and much of the soccer world—when he retired a few weeks after winning the FA Cup. Frantic fans tried to convince him to reconsider. The workers at one Liverpool factory even threatened to go on strike, but to no avail. Shankly summed up his legacy by remarking, "Above all, I would like to be remembered as a man who was selfless, who strove and worried so that others could share the glory, and who built up a family of people who could hold their heads up high and say, 'We're Liverpool.'"

THE STRING OF SUCCESS CONTINUES

The fans needn't have worried. Liverpool barely skipped a beat when Shankly's longtime assistant Bob Paisley assumed the reins. In a remarkable run, the team was first or second in the First Division from 1972–73 to 1979–80 and took back-to-back European Cup titles in 1977 and 1978. Players such as striker Kenny Dalglish, midfielder Graeme Souness, and defender Alan Hansen helped maintain Liverpool's superiority.

In 1980–81, the Reds finished fifth in First Division play but returned to the European Cup final for the third time in five years to face Real Madrid of Spain.

Midfielder Ray Kennedy's semifinal goal helped propel Liverpool to the 1981 European Cup final against Real Madrid.

Real had won the first five editions of the Cup, though this was the club's first finals appearance in 15 years. In a tight struggle, Liverpool's midfield and defense kept Real's attackers in check. In the 82nd minute, defender Alan Kennedy took a throw-in, dribbled through several defenders, and drilled a short left-footed drive from a sharp angle into the far corner of the net for a 1–0 triumph.

After a remarkable comeback the following season—Liverpool dipped to 11th place in late December yet rallied to win the First Division crown on the final day—Paisley called it a career. He had won at least one major trophy each year except his first. Striker Ian Rush helped give Paisley a memorable sendoff when he tallied four goals in a 5-0 rout over Everton in November 1982. Rush remains the only Reds player to notch

Bob Paisley hoisted his third European Cup in 1981.

a hat trick at Goodison Park, Everton's home pitch.

Liverpool continued its run of success under Joe Fagan, another Shankly protégé. The Reds won the League Cup—similar to the FA Cup but involving only the 92 teams in the Football League—and First Division in 1983–84, and then faced Roma of Italy in the European Cup. Liverpool took an early lead when Roma's keeper fumbled a shot on goal. The ball glanced off his head directly to fullback Phil Neal, who easily poked in a goal from about eight yards out. Roma tied the score just before halftime and dominated the second half, though neither team could score. For the first time ever, the Cup was decided by penalty kicks. With Liverpool ahead 3–2, keeper Bruce Grobbelaar twirled his legs in spaghetti-like contortions, which

Crowd riots at the 1985 European Cup marked a dark moment in Liverpool's history.

seemed to unnerve his foe. The ball struck the top of the crossbar and sailed into the stands. Moments later, Kennedy—the hero of three years earlier—sent the ball into the left corner of the net to clinch the win. The triumph made Liverpool the first English team to win three major competitions in the same season.

In an oddity, Liverpool was runner-up in five competitions during the 1984–85 season, including the First Division, Community Shield, Super Cup, and Club World Cup. The fifth competition, the 1985 European Cup, involved one of the major tragedies in European soccer history. Just before Liverpool took on Juventus of Italy, 39 Juventus fans died and hundreds more were injured in a stampede instigated by Liverpool supporters. Liverpool went on to lose 0–1.

Dalglish became player-manager when Fagan retired after just two seasons, and there was still no falloff in accomplishment. In 10 seasons under 3 managers (1981 to 1991), Liverpool won 6 First Division titles and placed second in the other 4.

There was, unfortunately, another tragedy involving the team in 1989, when Liverpool faced Nottingham Forest in the FA Cup semifinals at Hillsborough Stadium in Sheffield. Thousands of Liverpool supporters pressed forward into already crowded spectator areas. When a barrier broke, fans cascaded down on top of each other. Ninety-six people died in the crush, and nearly 800 were injured. The match was abandoned. Liverpool won the replay three weeks later, then it defeated Everton in the second all-Merseyside final in four years. Rush tallied twice for the Reds in the 3–2 win.

PLAYING IN THE PREMIER

In 1992, the top level of English soccer underwent a significant change with the formation of the Premier League. In essence, the new league replaced the First Division, though promotion and relegation continued as before.

Even though Liverpool had dominated the First Division up to that point, the Reds didn't do as well in succeeding years. Despite the best efforts of players such as striker Michael Owen—who led the Premier League in scoring during his first two years with the team and paced Liverpool for the next five—the team's best finish in the first decade was second place in 2001–02. It was especially galling that the Reds' great rivals, Manchester United, won an astonishing 13 titles in the new league's first 20 years.

The Reds, however, made their mark in other ways. In 2001, they won a cup treble. It began with a victory in the League Cup in February. In May, Liverpool defeated Arsenal 2–1 to take the FA Cup as Owen tallied twice in the final seven minutes. Four days later, the Reds hoisted the UEFA Cup after defeating Alavés of Spain in a wild 5–4 contest. The teams were tied 4–4 at the end of regulation time, and each had a goal disallowed in extra time because of an offside penalty. The game finally ended when Alavés defender Delfi Geli headed the ball into his own goal.

Perhaps Liverpool's most significant accomplishment during this era came in 2005 in the 50th edition of the European Cup, known as the Champions League

Steven Gerrard headed in a goal during the 2005 Champions League final, which became known as "The Miracle of Istanbul."

since 1992. After falling behind 3–0 to Italy's AC Milan at halftime of the final, Liverpool rallied to tie the score and won in a penalty shootout. The same teams met again two years later. This time, fortune favored the Italians, as Milan took a 2–0 lead into the game's final moments. A desperate Liverpool rally produced a goal by striker Dirk Kuyt with two minutes left, but Milan held on to win.

Sandwiched between those two games was the Reds' FA Cup victory in 2006. One of the most memorable moments of Liverpool's path to the final came during the fifth round. Liverpool defender John Arne Riise boomed a free kick so hard that it broke opposing midfielder Alan Smith's leg. Then, in the final against West Ham United, Gerrard's dramatic goal from 35 yards knotted the score at 3–3 with only seconds remaining. Keeper Pepe Reina blocked three of four West Ham penalty kicks, and Riise booted home the winner to give the Reds their seventh trophy. In 2012, the Reds also won their eighth League Cup to put them well ahead of the next closest team, Aston Villa, which had won the competition five times.

Liverpool came agonizingly close to its first Premier League title in 2013–14, riding an 11-game winning streak to a 5-point lead over Manchester City with 3 games remaining. But a loss to Chelsea, followed by a reversal of their 2005 "Miracle of Istanbul"—when the Reds tied Crystal Palace in the next-to-last game after giving up 3 goals in the final 10 minutes—resulted in a second-place finish by 2 points to Manchester City. Despite the disappointment, defender Martin Škrtel was optimistic. "I think that's a good experience for next season," he said. "I think there's quality in this team and that we can carry on this way for next season as well."

As has always been the case, Liverpool continues to generate outstanding young talent to complement its established stars. One exciting newcomer was winger Raheem Sterling, who joined the club in 2010. Early in 2014, English soccer columnist Scott Burns noted that Sterling had consistently improved to the point that he was "arguably the most in-form player in the Barclays Premier League." Another addition was defender Andre Wisdom, who captained the English under-21 team and signed with Liverpool when he was just 15. "He's a great young player, [has] shown a fantastic improvement, broken into the first team, and made a huge contribution," said Liverpool managing director Ian Ayre when Wisdom signed a long-term contract in 2013. "Getting talent like him to commit at this point is absolutely essential to the future." The team made a key acquisition in 2011, adding Uruguayan-born forward Luis Suárez. But with Suárez's transfer to Barcelona in 2014, the Reds looked to the leadership of longtime captain Gerrard and focused on strengthening their defense.

With its days of relegation only a distant, distasteful memory, Liverpool remained a Premier League fixture. Going forward, Kopites looked to push past traditional rivals Manchester United and Everton, as well as other powerhouses such as Arsenal, Chelsea, and Manchester City. As the Beatles might say, the Reds were "Getting Better" and felt confident that they would soon "Get Back" to the top of the Premier League.

Striker Luis Suárez, though a brilliant scorer, was more known for his controversial behavior.

MEMORABLE MATCHES

1892

Team was founded.

1895

Liverpool v. Newton Heath
Northwest Derby, October 12, 1895, Liverpool, England

Long before Newton Heath changed its name to Manchester United, it was one of Liverpool's greatest rivals. When the two teams met on a Saturday in 1895 in what would later become known as the Northwest Derby, the Reds got off to a fast start. Liverpool forward Frank Becton opened the scoring seven minutes into the game when he punched in a well-placed corner kick. Liverpool forwards Harry Bradshaw and Fred Geary added a goal each in the first half, though the "Heathens" (as Newton was commonly known) scored just before the break. Liverpool came back to shred the Newton Heath defense for three second-half scores as Geary, Bradshaw, and Becton each netted again. Then Liverpool forward Jimmy Ross, who had spent nearly the entire game setting up his teammates, scored the game's final goal despite being heavily guarded. The *Liverpool Mercury* noted, "It was a magnificent effort, and the crowd applauded it in no uncertain fashion." The 7–1 triumph remains the largest-ever margin of victory for the Reds in the long series between the two teams.

1965

Liverpool v. Leeds United

FA Cup Final, May 1, 1965, London, England

The 84th FA Cup final presented an intriguing matchup. Neither Liverpool nor Leeds had ever won, but the clubs seemed to be moving in opposite directions. After winning the First Division in 1963–64, Liverpool had fallen to seventh. Meanwhile, Leeds had soared from near-relegation to the Third Division to second place in the First Division in just three seasons and hoped to use the momentum in its first-ever finals appearance. Though Liverpool dominated, neither team scored in regulation time. The Reds took the lead three minutes into extra time when defender Gerry Byrne—who played almost the entire match with a broken collarbone—set up a header by striker Roger Hunt from about six yards out. Leeds responded to tie the score, but forward Ian St. John's diving header from point-blank range gave Liverpool its first-ever crown. "Grown men were crying, and it was the greatest feeling any human being could have to see what we had done," said manager Bill Shankly. "That was the greatest day, the one I treasure the most."

1977

Liverpool v. Borussia Mönchengladbach

European Cup Final, May 25, 1977, Rome, Italy

Playing in its first-ever European Cup final, Liverpool enjoyed the support of an estimated 25,000 fans who swarmed into Rome after overnight bus and train trips. Liverpool opened the scoring partway through the first half on a goal by midfielder Terry McDermott, but Mönchengladbach striker Allan Simonsen supplied the equalizer early in the second half. Liverpool regained the edge 12 minutes later when defender Tommy Smith headed in a corner kick. Liverpool removed any doubt of the outcome in the 82nd minute when forward Kevin Keegan was taken down hard in the penalty area. Defender Phil Neal slammed home the penalty kick, and Liverpool had its first European Cup with a 3–1 victory. After the match, Simonsen commented, "We didn't take Kevin Keegan seriously, and he had an excellent day. He was a good player, but on that day, he was amazing, and you could say he defeated us on his own." For manager Bob Paisley, the site of the triumph was especially fitting. While serving in the British Army in World War II, he had helped liberate Rome in 1944.

1985

Liverpool v. Juventus

European Cup Final, May 29, 1985, Brussels, Belgium

What happened in the stands of aging Heysel Stadium far overshadowed the on-pitch action of the 1985 European Cup final between Liverpool and Juventus. A chain-link fence separated supporters of the two teams, but both sides threw stones at each other before the match. Then, a mob of Liverpool fans swarmed across the flimsy barrier. Thousands of Juventus fans were jammed against a wall, which collapsed. Thirty-nine were killed and hundreds more injured. Fearing more violence if the game was canceled, officials allowed it to proceed. After a scoreless first half, Zbigniew Boniek of Juventus was judged to have been fouled just inside the penalty area by the referee trailing the play by at least 20 yards. (Replays seemed to indicate that the foul occurred while Boniek was still a step or two outside the penalty area.) Michel Platini drove the spot kick into the left corner of the goal for the game's only score as Liverpool keeper Bruce Grobbelaar dove in the opposite direction. Judging Liverpool to be at fault for the disaster, the UEFA suspended English teams from European Cup competition for five years.

1991

Liverpool v. Everton

Merseyside Derby, February 17, 20, and 27, 1991, Liverpool, England

Perhaps the most memorable Merseyside meeting came during the 1990–91 FA Cup. The teams battled to a scoreless tie at Everton, requiring a replay. The first half ended with Liverpool ahead 1–0. Everton pulled even a minute into the second half. With less than 20 minutes remaining, Liverpool scored, but Everton answered 2 minutes later. The Reds regained the lead four minutes afterward. In the waning moments, Everton knotted the score, and the game went into extra time. Again Liverpool took the lead, and again Everton responded. Everton's Tony Cottee, whose goal made the final score 4–4, said, "We had earned another replay, and the place went mad." His teammate Graeme Sharp added, "You talk to anyone about the game, and they said it was the best derby they'd ever seen." After the game, the Liverpool locker room erupted with screaming and finger-pointing. With all the stress, team manager Kenny Dalglish became concerned for his health and abruptly resigned. In the midst of the turmoil, the derby's second replay was almost an afterthought. Everton won 1–0.

2005

Liverpool v. AC Milan

Champions League Final, May 25, 2005, Istanbul, Turkey

Milan was heavily favored as the world's most prestigious club championship event celebrated its 50th anniversary. This optimism seemed justified when Milan's Paolo Maldini scored in the first minute. His teammate Hernán Crespo added a second goal at the 38-minute mark and a third just before halftime. "AC Milan is playing out of this world," said a British announcer. But in the second half, Liverpool brought the Italian club back to Earth in just six incredible minutes. First, Reds captain Steven Gerrard headed in a cross to put his team on the board, windmilling his arms to inspire the Liverpool faithful. Two minutes later, midfielder Vladimír Šmicer blasted in Liverpool's second goal from the edge of the box. Four minutes after that, Gerrard was fouled in the penalty area. Milan keeper Dida deflected defender Xabi Alonso's penalty kick, but the Spaniard knocked in the rebound to knot the score. The game went to a shootout when neither team could score again, and Liverpool won 3–2. At the beginning of the tournament, Reds fans had adopted "Make us dream" as their motto. The "Turkish Delight" victory in Istanbul was indeed a dream come true.

FAMOUS FOOTBALLERS

ELISHA SCOTT

(1893–1959)
Goalkeeper, 1912–34

Elisha Scott stood tall in goal, taller perhaps than any other Liverpool keeper—especially impressive since he was just 5-foot-9. A striker during his early teen years, Scott once ripped into his team's keeper. "What's the use of us scoring goals against the other team … my granny could be a better goalie than you!" he yelled. "Granny" found himself in goal the next game and stayed there throughout his career. Though he hoped to follow his older brother to Everton, the Blues deemed him too short, and he joined Liverpool. He went on to a career spanning 22 seasons—the longest in team history. He was especially noted for his rivalry with Everton's Dixie Dean, the most prolific scorer in English soccer history. According to a widely circulated story, when the two men passed each other on the streets of Liverpool, Dean would tap his hat—a reference to his skill in heading the ball. Scott would tumble to the ground, arms outstretched, as if he were making a save. More seriously, Dean said of his rival, "Elisha Scott, the Liverpool keeper, was the greatest I have ever seen."

JACK BALMER

(1916–84)
Striker, 1935–52

Jack Balmer seemed destined to play for Liverpool's Merseyside foe Everton. Two of his uncles had been Blues, and Balmer played two years as a teenaged amateur for Everton. The team made him a low-ball offer in 1935 to turn pro, but when Liverpool offered nearly double the money, he joined the Reds. Three years later, he scored the fastest goal in Liverpool history, just 10 seconds into the game—against Everton. Balmer carved an enduring niche out of the team's record book in 1946. After scoring hat tricks in two successive games, he netted twice in the following game, making fans clamor for another third goal. "No sooner had the words been spoken than [forward Harry] Eastham started the run which produced an angled chance for Balmer, who veered to the right and put the ball into the net to the biggest cheer Anfield had ever known in its long history," noted the *Liverpool Echo*. Two other First Division players had achieved the feat before Balmer, but none has since then. Unfortunately, Reds fans turned against him late in his career, seemingly because they didn't think he was aggressive enough.

ALBERT STUBBINS

(1919–2002)
Center-forward, 1946–53

Despite losing several years of his career to World War II, Albert Stubbins (pictured, right) made a strong impression on Liverpool fans. His 24 goals helped the team win the league championship in 1946–47, the Reds' first title in 24 years. Three of those goals came on March 1, 1947, when the Anfield pitch was covered with snow. One score began with a free kick from teammate Billy Liddell. As Stubbins said, "I started running at full speed. As the ball came flashing across, I just dived at it, and I was able to direct it to the keeper's left…. It just flew in! It was an icy ground, and both of my knees were lacerated and bleeding, but it was certainly worth it." Stubbins achieved enduring fame by appearing on the cover of the Beatles' 1967 album *Sgt. Pepper's Lonely Hearts Club Band*. Although John Lennon wasn't a soccer fan like Paul McCartney, he remembered Stubbins's name when the band was deciding who to put on the cover and liked it so much that he included him.

41

BOB PAISLEY

(1919–96)
Defender, 1939–54
Physiotherapist/reserve coach, 1954–59
Assistant manager, 1959–74
Manager, 1974–83

No one is more closely connected with Liverpool FC than Bob Paisley, who devoted nearly half a century to the team. World War II interrupted his career shortly after he signed, but he returned and served as a standout defender for a decade. After his playing days, he became a self-taught physiotherapist. Players marveled at his ability to diagnose problems simply by watching them walk a few steps. After 15 years as assistant manager to the legendary Bill Shankly, Paisley became a legend himself. "He ruled at Anfield with a rod of iron," said midfielder Graeme Souness. "If we looked as though we were becoming a little complacent, Bob would say, 'If you have all had enough of winning, come and see me, and I will sell the lot of you and buy 11 new players.' He meant it." In 1978, Paisley pointed out that, in its history, Liverpool had "won or been [runner-up] in the League, FA Cup, and European Cups 36 times. And I've been involved on 26 of those occasions, as player, assistant manager, or manager." He added five more trophies before retiring.

ROGER HUNT

(1938–)
Striker, 1958–69

Roger Hunt played a key role in the resurgence of Liverpool soccer from its eight years in the doldrums of the Second Division. Perhaps his best season was 1961–62, when he scored 41 goals in 41 games as Liverpool won the Second Division. His tally included five hat tricks and marked the first of eight consecutive years in which he led the team in scoring. He left after having scored 286 goals for the Reds, 245 of them in league competition—the latter still the team record as of 2014. He was also a member of the 1966 World Cup–winning English national team. Hunt's success was a testament to the value of hard work. "I knew perfectly well that I wasn't an out-and-out natural, the sort who can make a ball talk, so it was down to me to compensate for it in other ways," he said later. "I made up my mind that if I didn't succeed at Anfield, it wouldn't be for the lack of determination. From the first day, I threw myself into training, ran and tackled for everything, and practiced my ball skills at every opportunity."

STEVEN GERRARD

(1980–)
Midfielder, 1998–present

Steven Gerrard began his Liverpool career at the age of nine when he enrolled in the team's FC Academy. He signed his first contract at age 17, and gained full-time status 3 years later. Since then, he has become one of the most highly regarded players in all of soccer. According to ESPN FC, "Gerrard is a tireless runner and has superb vision. His striking from distance is feared around the world, and he is a prolific scorer for a midfielder." He became the first English-team player to score goals in four major finals: the FA Cup, League Cup, UEFA Cup, and Champions League. His Champions League goal in 2005 was especially memorable, igniting a Liverpool rally that carried the club to a seemingly impossible win over AC Milan. Gerrard is also noted for his leadership qualities, serving as captain both for Liverpool and the English national team. Gerrard even had a small acting role in *Will,* a 2011 film about the adventures of an 11-year-old Liverpool boy who travels to Istanbul, Turkey, to cheer on the team in the 2005 Champions League final.

LIVERPOOL FC TITLES
THROUGH 2014

**EUROPEAN CUP/
CHAMPIONS
LEAGUE**

Winner
1977
1978
1981
1984
2005
Total: 5

Runner-up
1985
2007
Total: 2

LEAGUE CUP

1981
1982
1983
1984
1995
2001
2003
2012
Total: 8

FOOTBALL LEAGUE FIRST DIVISION

1900–01
1905–06
1921–22
1922–23
1946–47
1963–64
1965–66
1972–73
1975–76
1976–77
1978–79
1979–80
1981–82
1982–83
1983–84
1985–86
1987–88
1989–90
Total: 18

FA CUP

1964–65
1973–74
1985–86
1988–89
1991–92
2000–01
2005–06
Total: 7

SELECTED BIBLIOGRAPHY

Goldblatt, David, and Johnny Acton. *The Soccer Book: The Sport, the Teams, the Tactics, the Cups.* New York: DK, 2010.

UEFA. *Champions of Europe, 1955–2005: 50 Years of the World's Greatest Club Football; The Best Goals from All 50 Finals.* DVD. Pleasanton, Calif.: Soccer Learning Systems, 2005.

Williams, John. *Red Men: Liverpool Football Club; the Biography.* Edinburgh: Mainstream, 2011.

Williams, John, and Stephen Hopkins. *The Miracle of Istanbul: Liverpool FC from Paisley to Benítez.* Edinburgh: Mainstream, 2006.

WEBSITES

LIVERPOOL FC

http://www.liverpoolfc.com/
Official website of Liverpool FC, including news, results,
features, videos, team history, and more.

PREMIER LEAGUE

http://www.premierleague.com/en-gb.html
The official Premier League website, with upcoming games, news and
features, standings, game and player photos, videos, and more.

Note: Every effort has been made to ensure that the websites listed above are suitable
for children, that they have educational value, and that they contain no inappropriate
material. However, because of the nature of the Internet, it is impossible to guarantee that
these sites will remain active indefinitely or that their contents will not be altered.

INDEX